FOUNDING THE AMERICAN COLONIES

FOUNDING THE
AMERICAN COLONIES
DIANA REISCHE

Franklin Watts
New York/London/Toronto/Sydney
A First Book/1989

For Eric and Kirk,
whose ancestors signed
the Mayflower Compact

Cover photograph courtesy of The Bettmann Archive

Photographs courtesy of The Granger Collection:
pp. 8, 11, 15 (top and bottom), 20 (top), 22 (bottom),
24, 30 (bottom), 34, 40 (top and bottom), 46 (top and
bottom), 52 (top and bottom), 57 (bottom), 61 (top
and bottom); Library of Congress: p. 20 (bottom);
The Bettmann Archive: p. 22 (top); New York Public
Library Picture Collection: pp. 30 (top), 57 (top).

Library of Congress Cataloging in Publication Data

Reische, Diana L.
Founding the American colonies / by Diana Reische.
p.   cm. — (A First book)
Bibliography: p.
Includes index.
Summary: Describes the founding, problems, and social and economic
survival of the original thirteen American colonies.
ISBN 0-531-10686-1
1. United States — History — Colonial period, ca. 1600-1775 —
Juvenile literature. [1. United States — History — Colonial period,
ca. 1600-1775.] I. Title. II. Series.
E191.R45   1989
973.2 — dc19   88-30343   CIP   AC

CONTENTS

FOUNDING THE AMERICAN COLONIES

THE PORTRAICTUER OF CAPTAYNE IOHN SMITH ADMIRALL OF NEW ENGLAND.

Captain John Smith, first leader
of the Jamestown colony

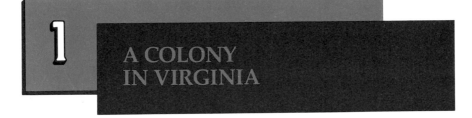

A COLONY IN VIRGINIA

A boy with the very ordinary name of John Smith grew up in an ordinary English farm family. Yet he dreamed of fighting Spaniards and having adventures. When John was thirteen, he heard that the famous English sea captain Sir Francis Drake was about to sail again. He begged his father to let him sign on. Instead, his father took him to a merchant to learn a trade.

Four years later, John ran off to fight in wars in Europe. Before long, he was *Captain* John Smith, with many adventures to tell. Once he was tossed off a ship and left to drown, but he saved himself by joining a pirate crew.

No wonder that when a London company needed a fearless soldier for a risky trip, they chose twenty-seven-year-old Captain Smith. The adventure was to settle America.

The London Company was one of two new firms that had permission of the English king, James I, to start colonies. One company had the right to settle the north coast of America. The London Company (soon renamed the Virginia Company) got the rights to the southern coast.

At the time, the only European colony in what is now the United States was Spain's settlement at St. Augustine, Florida. Why were there no other colonies? Columbus had discovered the Americas more than one hundred years earlier. Many people tried to start colonies. But each one had failed.

England and most of Europe had been busy fighting wars. They couldn't spare the ships or money to start settlements. Then in 1604, Spain and England signed a peace treaty. Now the English could think seriously about starting colonies.

In December 1606, three ships—the *Discovery,* the *Sarah Constant,* and the *Goodspeed*—left London with 144 men and boys aboard. Winter storms battered them. Everyone seemed to be sick or quarrelling. When the ships got to the Chesapeake Bay in April, 105 people had lived through the winter crossing. On May 14, 1607, they began a settlement

*The first English colonists in America
at Jamestown, Virginia*

called Jamestown on the James River. Both the town and the river were named for King James I.

Who were these colonists? One list mentions four carpenters, one surgeon, a blacksmith, two bricklayers, a mason, a minister, a tailor, twelve laborers, a drummer, and four boys. At least a third of them were "gentlemen" who had never done a day's work and didn't plan to start now. They expected to get rich quickly in Virginia. Smith wrote of them that there was "no talk, no hope, nor work, but dig gold, wash gold, refine gold, load gold." They talked of gold but didn't find a speck of it.

As they hunted for gold, the colonists swatted mosquitoes. Jamestown was built in swampy land. Diseases killed first one man, then another. People fought constantly. Little work got done.

While others grumbled, Smith went scouting and made friends with the Indians. He suggested that the settlers try the Indian way of planting corn, but the gentlemen laughed. What did a low-born soldier know of such things?

Food ran out that winter. When a supply ship with more colonists arrived in January, only thirty-eight of the first group were still alive.

That fall, the settlers asked Captain Smith to take charge. He forced them to stop griping and start working.

"He that will not work shall not eat," he said. He had them plant corn the Indian way and dig a well to get pure water. Almost everyone made it through that winter.

Then new tragedy struck. A spark set fire to Smith's gunpowder pouch. Badly burned, he had to return to England. Once again, the settlers fought among themselves.

In 1609, the company sent four hundred new settlers, but the ships got caught in storms. Four hundred people finally stumbled ashore, sick from eating spoiled food. Instead of good food and healthy workers, here were more sick, hungry people!

The next months are known as the "starving time." The settlers had lost the Indians' friendship. They didn't dare go beyond the fence to hunt or gather wood. They ate dogs, rats, and even chewed on leather to try to keep from starving. Only about sixty people lived through that terrible winter.

The colonists wanted to leave. In June 1610, they boarded a ship for England. As they floated down the James River, they saw sails. The arriving ships brought supplies, three hundred colonists, and a new governor, Lord De la Warr.

Lord De la Warr set up a tough army system. Men were ranked from privates to captains. Twice a day, to the beat of drums, they marched to church. They marched to work. Anyone who did not obey orders was punished.

No one was happy about Jamestown. Army life wasn't what the settlers had expected. Some colonists ran away and joined the Indians. Some escaped on passing ships. The company's owners were also unhappy. So far the colony had not made a penny for them.

Finally, one of the colonists, John Rolfe, found a way to grow a mild tobacco that sold well in England. With this cash crop, Virginia's future looked better. In fact, so much money could be made in tobacco that colonists planted too much of it. They forgot to plant enough food because they were too busy growing tobacco.

John Rolfe helped Jamestown in another way when he married Pocahontas. His marriage to the daughter of the most important Indian chief brought peace with the Indians for several years.

Virginia began to grow. A second settlement was started many miles up the James River at what is now Richmond. By 1616, Virginia had eight villages along its rivers. At first everyone worked for

Above: *English ships being loaded with tobacco grown in Virginia.* Below: *the marriage of Pocahontas and John Rolfe in April 1614.*

the company, which owned all the land. A new governor decided to let people have private gardens. These gardens began to solve the food problem. People worked harder on their own land.

The company could not find enough people to send to the colony because people in England had heard about the suffering in Jamestown. The company decided to offer free land to draw more settlers.

By 1619, Virginia had grown large enough to need a local government. Each district elected two people as burgesses, or representatives of the people. (*Burgess* is an old word for freeman.) On July 30, 1619, twenty-two burgesses met in Jamestown's church to make laws. The governor could ignore their laws. Yet it was a start on self-government in the colonies.

Virginia's problems were not over. The Indians had become upset because so many English were moving into their hunting and fishing grounds. In 1622, Indians killed 347 colonists. In the war that followed, farmers could not work their fields. People went hungry once again.

More than five thousand people had come to Virginia over an eighteen-year period, but in 1624, Virginia still had only about twelve hundred colonists. Yet the colony survived and grew. Through trial and error, settlers learned hard lessons about how to live in a wilderness. Every later colony learned something from Virginia.

By 1624, another band of colonists was settling land explored by Smith. It was far to the north, in a place he named New England.

2 PILGRIMS AND PURITANS OF MASSACHUSETTS

What was the future governor of Plymouth colony doing hanging upside down in a tree? He was exploring, that was what, and he had stepped into an Indian deer trap. The bent tree snagged him and flipped him into the air. William Bradford was part of a scouting party off the ship *Mayflower*.

Back on ship others waited for news. Where should they settle? Everyone knew they were not where they were supposed to be. They had permission to start a colony in northern Virginia. Instead, they were off the coast of New England.

The *Mayflower*'s captain refused to sail down the coast to Virginia. It was too dangerous in winter. They would have to stay here. They knew where they were, for Captain John Smith had mapped this coast after he left Jamestown. They were off the upper tip of Cape Cod, Massachusetts.

Captain Miles Standish put on his breastplate armor to lead exploring parties. Across Cape Cod Bay they found a protected harbor at Plymouth. It had cleared fields and fresh water. They dug up buried baskets of Indian corn. On Christmas Day, they began to build their colony.

Who were these colonists? Their story goes back to England many years before. By law, people in England had to support the Church of England. The group on the *Mayflower* was part of a much larger group that wanted to change the Church of England. They wanted to make it simpler. Because they wanted to "purify" the church, they were called Puritans.

After some Puritans were jailed and a few put to death, one group fled to Holland. They were called Pilgrims, because they had left their homes to practice their faith. After ten years in Holland, some worried that their children were growing up Dutch instead of English. These Pilgrims got a patent from the London Company to settle in northern Virginia.

About forty Pilgrims arrived in London to make the dangerous trip. To fill out the group, the company hired some Londoners to go along. John

The Mayflower *approaching the coast of Massachusetts in 1620.*

The Pilgrims landing at Plymouth in December 1620.

Smith spoke to the Pilgrims about becoming their military leader, but they turned him down. They said they didn't need him because they already had his maps and his book about the American coast. Instead of Smith, they hired a short, hot-tempered captain named Miles Standish.

They hoped to leave in April and arrive in time to plant crops, but it was September before the *Mayflower* left London. Those on board weren't rich or well-born. They were farmers and craftspeople who were used to hard work. There were fifty men, twenty women, and thirty-four children and babies among them.

When the ship landed in the wrong place, some of the Londoners began to talk boldly. They claimed that they did not have to obey the company's rules since they were not in Virginia. The Pilgrims drew up a compact, or agreement, and asked every adult male to sign it. The Mayflower Compact said the signers would form a government. Signers promised to obey the "just and equal" laws of the community. On November 21, 1620, forty-one men signed the Compact. Then they elected Deacon John Carver, a London merchant, as governor and went ashore.

They carried muskets and swords in case of Indian attack, but they met few Indians. Diseases

had nearly wiped out the Indian population. That was why the Pilgrims found cleared fields but no people at Plymouth.

The Pilgrims sawed boards for tiny houses as a cold December rain fell. They cut reeds for thatched roofs. The largest building, the church, served as both a meeting house and a fort.

Whole families died that winter. Short of food, living in partially built huts, they were too weak and cold to fight off illness. All pitched in to help the others. When Governor Carver died, the Pilgrims chose Bradford to take his place.

As soon as the ground thawed in the spring, they planted peas, wheat, beans, and corn. They were just starting this job when an Indian walked up and greeted them in English. Squanto had been kidnapped many years earlier and taken to England. He showed the Pilgrims how to find shellfish and make fish traps. He taught them a better way to plant corn and how to grow pumpkin.

Above: *the signing of the Mayflower Compact.*
Below: *building in winter.*

Squanto teaching the Pilgrims how to plant corn

An Indian named Samoset also helped the Pilgrims. He took them to meet Massasoit, chief of the Wampanoags. Governor Bradford made the colonists treat the Indians fairly and politely. When the Pilgrims harvested their first crops in the fall of 1621, they asked Massasoit and his people to join them in a feast of thanksgiving.

In November 1621, the ship *Fortune* arrived with thirty-five new settlers and a patent from the Council of New England. The patent gave them the legal right to be just where they were.

The community grew from one street to two. There were still no cattle and only a few chickens, but the settlers had nets to catch striped bass and cod. They found lobsters and clams. They dreamed of bread but couldn't make it without wheat. Women couldn't make jams from the berries they picked because they had no sugar.

Two ships brought about ninety more people in 1623. Many were wives, children, and friends from Holland. The newcomers gasped when they saw the thin, ragged Plymouth settlers. It was a year before another ship arrived with three cows and a bull, the first cattle in New England.

Like Jamestown, Plymouth needed something to sell so that the settlers could buy needed supplies. They made deals with Indians to trade corn, beads, and tools for fur. Soon Plymouth was shipping beaver and otter skins to England. Plymouth even started a trading post in what is now the state of Maine.

In 1630, when Plymouth had about three hundred people, ships arrived with a thousand newcomers. They were also Puritans. Led by Governor John Winthrop, this group held a charter to start a Massachusetts Bay Colony. They began the town of Boston in a harbor up the coast from Plymouth. Massachusetts Bay grew fast, partly because the company offered settlers free land. By 1640, there were villages at Salem, Marblehead, Newbury, Ipswich, Gloucester, Watertown, Newton, and other places.

The Puritans believed it was a sin to waste time, so they worked very hard. They raised cattle. They built ships for trade and for the fishing industry starting up at Salem. They made cloth. And they spread out. People from Massachusetts founded settlements up and down the coast. By 1640, the New England region had a population of at least twenty thousand. Virginia and the new colony of Maryland together had less than ten thousand.

3 MARYLAND: A SAFE PLACE FOR CATHOLICS

A shipload of corn reached Massachusetts in 1634 from Maryland, a colony that was only a year old. Settlers from Maryland swapped the corn for salted cod. Unlike Jamestown and Plymouth, Maryland did not have a "starving time." The settlers came with enough food and farm animals. The colony's founder kept them well supplied.

Lord Baltimore wasn't just Maryland's founder. He owned it right down to the last strawberry vine. Yet he did not start a colony just to make money. He started it partly because of religious problems in England. Catholics could not go to mass openly. They had to pay fines for not belonging to the Church of England.

George Calvert, Lord Baltimore, was a Catholic who feared the growing power of the Puritans. He decided to leave England to start a colony in North America. He tried first in Newfoundland. Soon, however, he wrote to King Charles I, "I am determined to [leave] this place to fishermen." Lord Baltimore wrote Charles that he was heading for Virginia and "hoped your Majesty will please to grant me . . . land there." That is just what happened in 1632, when Charles granted him land north of the Potomac River.

Calvert never saw it, for he died that year. To his twenty-six-year-old son Cecil Calvert went more than ten million acres of land and the title of Lord Baltimore. The land included all of what is now Maryland, Delaware, bits of Virginia, Pennsylvania, and West Virginia. Under the grant, the Lord Proprietor, or owner, could collect taxes, wage war, grant titles, make laws, and set up courts.

Lord Baltimore named his brother, Leonard Calvert, governor. The new colony was named Maryland in honor of Queen Henrietta Maria, the Catholic wife of King Charles I.

The first Lord Baltimore had promised the king that Protestants would not be harmed even though the colony was run by Catholics. When the ships *Ark* and *Dove* sailed for the colony, they carried more Protestants than Catholics. Most of the Protestants were servants.

With 220 colonists aboard, the ships reached the mouth of the Potomac River in early spring of 1634. Instead of building a new settlement, the colonists bought an Indian village near the river. The Indians had planned to move anyway and were happy to sell the whole place—wigwams, fields, and all for axes, hatchets, hoes, and cloth. Then the settlers set to work planting and building. They built houses, a fort, a mill, and a chapel shared by Protestants and Catholics. Leonard Calvert and other gentlemen worked alongside their servants. Women and children collected the land's bounty: strawberries, walnuts, and hickory nuts.

If they needed supplies, it was only a short boat ride to the Virginia settlements. But the Calverts had made sure that their "adventurers" arrived with the gear needed on the frontier. Lord Baltimore suggested that each man bring three suits, three shirts, six pairs of shoes, and three pairs of stockings. He told each household to bring a rug for a bed cover, two pairs of canvas sheets, and canvas to make a mattress stuffed with husks.

Calvert promised each person who paid his own passage 100 acres (40 ha) of land. Someone who brought five men got about 2,000 acres (800

Sir George Calvert, Lord Baltimore

The first Catholic Mass being held in Maryland

ha). Those who got property agreed to pay a small yearly rent "forever" to the Calverts.

The colony did well as planters harvested tobacco from the rich soil. Yet people worried. In 1642, civil war broke out in England. A Puritan army fought the king's forces. What would happen to the colony if the Puritans won?

To protect both Catholics and Protestants, Lord Baltimore wrote a law called the Toleration Act. It said that no Christian could be harmed for his or her beliefs. Maryland was the first colony to grant religious freedom to its citizens.

While England ripped itself apart with war, dozens of new settlements were founded along the American coast from Virginia to Maine.

4 OUT FROM MASSACHUSETTS: CONNECTICUT AND NEW HAMPSHIRE

A ship from Plymouth sailed up the Connecticut River in 1633. It was carrying materials to build a trading post. The chiefs of two Indian tribes had visited Massachusetts to invite colonists to the Connecticut Valley. The chiefs wanted to trade furs. They also hoped the settlers could drive the warlike Pequot tribe out of the valley.

Some Europeans were already there. Dutch from the colony of New Netherland claimed the valley. Only three months earlier, the Dutch had built a trading fort on the river. The fort was supposed to keep the English out.

"Strike your colors, or we will fire upon you," the Dutch commander shouted as the little ship from Plymouth neared.

"I have the commission of the Governor of Plymouth to go up the river and I shall go," Lieutenant William Holmes replied.

Holmes sailed past the fort's two cannons, but the Dutch held their fire. Six miles (10 km) upriver, the Plymouth Pilgrims began a settlement called Windsor. The Dutch commander sent for help, but it was a month before soldiers got there. By that time the Pilgrims had built a fence around Windsor, and the Dutch decided not to fight.

That same year, John Oldham followed Indian paths from Massachusetts Bay to the Connecticut Valley. He returned two years later to start a town, Wethersfield, just below the Dutch outpost. Now there were English both upriver and downriver from the Dutch.

The new settlements were part of a wave of people leaving Massachusetts. Some of the settlements were founded by religious rebels and some by fishermen, traders, or farmers. Between 1629 and 1638, five New England colonies were started— Connecticut, Maine, New Hampshire, New Haven, and Rhode Island.

Some settlements were begun because people didn't like the way Massachusetts Bay was run. Governor John Winthrop and the Puritan ministers made all sorts of rules that people had to obey, such

*Thomas Hooker and his congregation
on their way to Connecticut*

as having to go to church on Sundays and not danc-ing. If a person didn't agree with these men, Mas-sachusetts could be very uncomfortable.

The Reverend Thomas Hooker was a Puritan, but he didn't agree with them. Hooker thought people should have more say in their government. He wanted to give ordinary people, not just those picked by church leaders, a vote.

Hooker and the people in his church headed west. They, too, chose the fertile Connecticut Val-ley. Meadows with good grazing for their cattle and good soil for growing crops were there. In 1636, Hooker and thirty-five families walked for two weeks through deep forests to the site that is now Hartford. Their settlement became the center of a group of river villages. Three towns formed the Connecticut colony in 1636.

If Hooker thought the Massachusetts Bay Col-ony was too rigid, another minister thought it too easygoing. The Reverend John Davenport planned a place run on very strict Puritan ideas. Davenport led his followers to the shore of the Long Island Sound, where they founded New Haven. In New Haven, only church members could vote or hold office. New Haven was taken over by Connecticut in 1665.

While settlers chopped trees to clear land for farms and villages, back in England the king and the stock companies kept handing out land grants. Often the new grants gave away land that had already been given to someone else. People in England weren't too clear about what was where in America.

In 1622, the king gave Sir Fernando Gorges and John Mason the right to start a colony in northern New England. Their grant was called the "main" (Maine) because it was on the mainland of a coast dotted by islands. Gorges and Mason split up their holdings. Gorges took Maine, and Mason kept the southern part. Maine did not last as a separate colony. It was taken over by Massachusetts and remained part of Massachusetts until 1820.

Meanwhile, Mason named his colony New Hampshire in 1629. Others had already settled there. Probably the first settlers were a small group led in 1623 by David Thomson. They founded a fishing and timbering settlement at a site the Indians called "the place where three rivers make one," Piscataqua. Edward and William Hilton began a fishing village that became Dover.

Mason died in 1635, leaving New Hampshire to his grandson, a child. With no leader, the tiny colony went through several bad years and in 1641 agreed to become part of Massachusetts. New Hampshire again became a separate colony in 1680.

5 RHODE ISLAND: A MAGNET FOR REBELS

Massachusetts officials sent a ship to Salem with orders to seize a pesky minister and pack him off to England. Before he could be captured, someone warned Roger Williams, and he escaped. Who alerted him? It was probably the governor of Massachusetts, John Winthrop. Though they disagreed often, the two men were friends all their lives.

Roger Williams was like that. He was always arguing and disagreeing, but he was so charming and so brilliant that even when he made people furious, they still liked him. And he made a lot of people furious.

At first, Boston's leaders had welcomed the gifted young minister. In fact, they asked him to speak in the Boston church. To their surprise, he refused. He objected because the Boston church wasn't completely separated from the Church of England. It was Puritan, but it was not Puritan enough for Williams. Winthrop warned his young friend to be a bit less blunt.

Williams moved to Salem, then Plymouth, then Salem again. In each place his ideas caused an uproar. He said King James had no right to grant land in the colonies since the land belonged to the Indians. By saying he could give away the land, the king "told a solemn public lie." The Plymouth colony had enough problems without a minister who called the king a liar. They asked Williams to leave.

In Salem, Williams alarmed people by preaching that church and state should be separate. The church should not have any say in running Massachusetts, he said. And he said the government should not support any one church. That was a bombshell. The whole point of the Massachusetts Bay colony was that it was a Puritan government. Church and state were totally linked. Williams' views questioned the whole setup. He argued that no one should be forced to go to church, as they were in Massachusetts and Plymouth. "Forced worship stinks in God's nostrils," he said.

Though people liked him, he had gone too far. In 1635, Massachusetts leaders sent a ship to capture him, but Williams slipped away into the forest. He headed south to lands controlled by the Wampanoags. Through the winter, he lived with Indians, learning their language and customs.

In the spring, Williams went to Narragansett Bay. There he started Providence Plantations, which became Rhode Island. It was an illegal colony as far as England was concerned. He had no land grant and no patent from the king or a land company.

The little settlement drew many other rebels. People from his Salem church and others followed Williams. They built a village of thatch-roofed houses below a cliff. On the ridge above, they planted gardens and fruit trees. Williams gave every settler five acres (2 ha) for a garden and six acres (2 ha) for cornfields.

Williams let everyone practice his or her religion freely. Maryland had already passed laws that protected Christians. Williams went even further by saying that all people, not just Christians, had the right to follow their own faith.

While Williams was founding a colony based on freedom of religion, Massachusetts tossed out another rebel thinker. Anne Hutchinson's crime was that she held prayer meetings and commented on sermons. In 1638, her family and followers headed

Above: *the Indians helped Roger Williams during his journey to Rhode Island.*

Left: *Anne Hutchinson on trial in Boston in 1637.*

for Providence. Williams helped them buy land from the Indians at what is now Portsmouth.

One of her followers, the merchant William Coddington, started Newport a year later. Samuel Gorton started the community of Warwick after his family left Plymouth. Gorton had fallen out with Plymouth's leaders when he spoke up for his wife's maid in court. Her crime? She had smiled in church.

Long before Rhode Island got its patent as a colony in 1644, Anne Hutchinson had moved to the only other northern colony that welcomed people of different religions, Dutch New Netherland.

6 NEW NETHERLAND AND NEW SWEDEN

Six years before the Pilgrims reached Plymouth, the Dutch built a trading fort far up the Hudson River at what is now Albany. It was a fine place to trade with the Indians for beaver, sable, and other furs. When the trading post was built, the only North American colonies were Jamestown, French Quebec in Canada, and Spanish St. Augustine in Florida.

Though they began colonizing early, the Dutch were not mainly interested in settlements. Trading companies built the Dutch outposts. Their main goal was to make money. The Dutch West India Company was formed in 1621, a year after the Pilgrims reached Plymouth. The company built forts on the rivers claimed by the Netherlands for the new Dutch colony of New Netherland.

At home, the company tried to find people willing to settle in America. That was a big problem. Holland was such a good place to live that few Dutch wanted to leave.

A group of about thirty families finally sailed for New Netherland in 1624. They brought seeds for wheat, barley, and rye and materials for a grist mill. Some of the group settled on what is now Governor's Island in New York harbor. Others went to the river forts.

Two years later a new director-general of the company, Peter Minuit, made a famous land deal. He gave a group of Indians trinkets worth about $24 for the island of Manhattan. There Minuit started a town, New Amsterdam.

Three ships arrived that year. The *Cow,* the *Sheep,* and the *Horse* carried just what you might guess—animals. The Dutch Colony had enough food right from the beginning.

Business was brisk as the Dutch made deals with Indians to swap muskets and other goods for furs. Still, the company could not attract many Dutch settlers. The colony therefore welcomed people from other colonies and countries. Unlike the stern New England villages, New Amsterdam was an easygoing seaport with more taverns than churches. In 1643, when a French priest visited, he heard eighteen different languages. He met not only Dutch but Swedes, English, French, Portuguese, Italians, Danes, and many others.

The Dutch also settled Brooklyn, Long Island, Staten Island, the Bronx, and the town of Yonkers up the Hudson River. In each place, there were likely to be as many non-Dutch as Dutch. Some English people who were unhappy with Puritan rule in New England moved to the Dutch colony. Even so, New Netherland grew very slowly.

The company offered anyone who would bring fifty or more settlers the right to buy huge pieces of land. The owners were called patroons—Dutch for lords of the manor. Patroons had great power. They acted as judge and jury in cases on their lands. Workers could not leave the property without the patroon's permission.

The patroon system did not draw many settlers. People could get free land elsewhere. Why work for a patroon? The company decided to let anyone who brought five people to the colony buy 200 acres (80 ha) of land from the Indians. But since it was easier to get free land in the English colonies, people still had little reason to go to New Netherland.

Governor Willem Kieft, who took over in 1637, hated Indians. He ordered a mass killing of Indians in 1644 that led to an uprising. Indians attacked every settlement in the Dutch colony.

In 1646, a one-legged Dutch hero named Peter Stuyvesant arrived to bring order. Indians called him "Old Silver Leg" for the silver decorations on his wooden leg.

Meanwhile, former governor Minuit angered the Dutch by starting a colony on lands claimed by the Netherlands. Minuit helped start a Swedish trading company to compete with the Dutch in North America.

The first two Swedish ships bringing colonists reached the Delaware River in 1638. Some miles up the river, they built Fort Christina, named for the twelve-year-old Swedish queen. The site is now Wilmington, Delaware.

Many of New Sweden's colonists actually came from Finland. Not many Swedes seemed to want to leave their homeland. In fact, New Sweden never did get enough settlers. When the Dutch decided to capture the Swedish colony, there were too few Swedish colonists to stop them. In 1655, "Old Silver Leg" Stuyvesant captured New Sweden for the Dutch.

For New Netherland and all the North American colonies, far-off wars brought changes. The English Civil War ended with the execution of Charles I. A period of Puritan rule followed. Then, in 1660, Charles II got back the English throne his father had lost. The new king gave his brother New Netherland. The fact that England didn't own it didn't bother him. England and the Netherlands had become enemies.

That is why, in 1664, four English ships sailed into the New Amsterdam harbor. Governor John Winthrop, Jr., of Connecticut, son of the famous Massachusetts governor, was aboard and called on Stuyvesant to turn the colony over to England. The tough old Dutch soldier wanted to fight, but leading citizens asked him to give up. So ended Dutch control of what are now New York, New Jersey, and Delaware.

Above: *Peter Minuit trading with Indians for the island of Manhattan.* Below: *Peter Stuyvesant at New Amsterdam.*

7

CHARLES II DRAWS NEW MAPS

When the English invaded New Amsterdam, the king was busy reshaping the colonies. Charles II created five new English colonies between 1660 and 1684—New York, New Jersey, Pennsylvania, Delaware, and Carolina. He did it partly to repay people who had helped him get back his throne. When Charles II was crowned, his family had been out of power for years. He owed money and favors to those who had backed him while Puritans ruled England. He rewarded some people by giving them American colonies.

To his brother James, the Duke of York, Charles gave the most land. As Lord High Admiral, York was too busy building up the English navy to fight the Dutch and Spanish to visit his new American holdings. They included everything between the Connecticut and Delaware rivers, plus what are now New Jersey, Delaware, New York, part of Maine, and the islands of Martha's Vineyard and Nantucket. The Lord High Admiral sent a fleet in 1664 to claim his colony, which he called New York. The colony surrendered without a fuss.

Meanwhile, the Duke of York repaid some debts of his own. In 1664, he gave George Carteret and John Berkeley part of the old Dutch colony west of the Hudson River. They named it New Jersey after Carteret's home on the island of Jersey.

There were small settlements of Dutch and Swedes in New Jersey. One was the Dutch village of Bergen (now Jersey City). A few former New Englanders also worked farms in Jersey's rich soil.

In 1665, the new owners sent thirty colonists to build Elizabethtown as capital of New Jersey. Many more people soon arrived from New England and from England, Ireland, and Scotland. Newark, Shrewsbury, Middletown, Woodbridge, and Piscataway all began within three years.

Lord Berkeley sold his share of New Jersey in 1674 to two English Quakers, members of a church called the Society of Friends. The Quakers formed the separate colony of West Jersey. Carteret's half became East Jersey.

West Jersey drew many Quakers who had left England because they could not practice their religion freely there. West Jersey passed laws in 1677 that protected religious freedom. The laws also forbade jailing people for debts and set up an assembly elected by secret ballot. The two Jerseys stayed separate until 1702, when they were united once again as New Jersey.

Berkeley didn't give up all his American holdings when he sold half of New Jersey. In 1663, Charles gave him and seven other people land known as Carolina. It stretched from Virginia into Spanish Florida. To use the southern part, colonists might have to fight the Spanish, who also claimed it.

The new Lords Proprietor faced other problems. They didn't have good maps or descriptions of Carolina. Except for small farms on the Virginia border, Europeans had not been able to live there. Many had tried but failed. Some settlers had built houses in unhealthy places or did not have enough supplies. Other settlers were driven off by Indians. Spain had tried to start a colony at Parris Island but failed. France failed at Port Royal. A colony at Roanoke Island failed twice. A group from Massachusetts settled at the mouth of Cape Fear River. Before they gave up and left, they tacked a sign up that said the place was useless for settlement.

The new owners hired William Hilton to explore. His ship was caught in terrifying storms, but he brought back good news. He said thousands of English could make a living in Carolina.

Anthony Ashley Cooper, the Earl of Shaftesbury, talked the other owners into putting up more money. With the funds, they printed pamphlets telling of Carolina's wonders. They said any woman who came was sure to find a husband. The owners offered 100 acres (40 ha) of free land to heads of families and more for those with servants. They also promised religious freedom.

The first successful Carolina settlers left England in 1670. They chose a site not far from what is now Charleston and named it Charles Town. They soon decided to move Charles Town to a peninsula where the Ashley and Cooper rivers meet. The new town had a fine sheltered harbor and was a perfect spot for a port city.

To the settlement came French Protestants, Scottish Presbyterians, and English of many religions. Spanish ships attacked several times, but the people of Charles Town fought them off.

At Lord Shaftesbury's orders, colonists set out

*King
Charles II
of England.*

*Anthony
Ashley
Cooper, the
Earl of
Shaftesbury.*

test plantings to see what would grow best. They planted orange, lemon, lime, fig, and date trees. They tried tropical fruits and tobacco, potatoes and cotton, flax and grape vines. Hogs and cattle did so well that Carolina sold meat to the West Indies. Someone planted rice in nearby swamps and found a crop just meant for the hot, soggy land.

Many of Charles Town's settlers came from Barbados, a port in the West Indies slave trade. The settlers began buying black slaves to work the new rice plantations. By 1708, blacks outnumbered whites in South Carolina. The colony's economy was based on the work of slaves.

Northern Carolina grew much more slowly. The north lacked a good seaport. Though free land was offered, colonists had to pay the colony's owners a yearly fee. It was cheaper to own land in Virginia, so why go to Carolina? For many years, there were only small settlements of tobacco farmers in the Albemarle region.

The independent people who moved into the north mostly ignored the governor 300 miles (480 km) away in Charles Town. Finally, the owners split Carolina in two. North Carolina became a separate colony in 1712. But before that happened, Charles had created two more colonies.

8 PENN'S COLONIES: PENNSYLVANIA AND DELAWARE

One of the Duke of York's friends was a charming lawyer, a fine businessman, and a natural leader. Yet William Penn was also a missionary for the Society of Friends, or Quakers. English laws were very hard on Quakers. A judge gave Penn a choice: give up his religion or go to jail for the rest of his life. Penn went to prison, but the king freed him.

Penn's father, a famous admiral, had helped the king win back the throne. He had also loaned Charles a fortune. Since Penn was his father's heir, the king owed him the money. Even though the younger Penn was an outspoken Quaker, the king and his brother liked him. When Penn preached against luxury and having fun, the fun-loving king didn't get angry.

Penn studied maps of land west of the Delaware River. Then he asked the king to give him those lands to repay the old debt. Charles didn't bother to pay many of his debts, but he agreed to this. In 1681, the king granted Penn the colony of Pennsylvania, Penn's Woods. Looking at the maps again, Penn saw that he didn't have a good seaport. Pennsylvania was inland. Ships arriving in the Delaware Bay might stop before they got to Pennsylvania. One possible port was New Castle, which belonged to the Duke of York. Penn asked him for it, and York gave him the counties that later became Delaware.

As Lord Proprietor, Penn could choose officials, lay out towns, and write his beliefs into law. As he made laws for the two colonies, Penn quoted the Golden Rule, "Do unto others as ye would have others do unto you."

He planned great estates for wealthy landowners like himself. But he had lived on his father's estates in Ireland, where the poor owned almost nothing. He didn't want to repeat Ireland's errors. Penn offered free land to people who brought servants with them. When a servant's indenture, or time of service, ran out, the servant got free land.

Penn wanted people to be free to worship as they chose. The Quaker colony was opened to people of many faiths. In 1682, Penn issued a Frame of Government, which guaranteed freedom of religion and trial by jury.

For his capital city, Philadelphia, Penn wanted a "green country town." It was laid out in broad squares set between two rivers.

Like the owners of Carolina, Penn printed pamphlets to get people to come to his colony. The pamphlets gave honest facts about travel costs, climate, and what it would be like to live in the colony. Pamphlets and ads in England, Scotland, Wales, Germany, and Holland drew sixty shiploads of settlers to Philadelphia in one year alone, 1683.

The newcomers wrote home of buying good land at low cost. They reported that officials did not insist on any one religion. More people arrived. Quakers came from Wales, Ireland, and England. To Lancaster County came members of German religious groups, such as the Amish and Mennonites.

Above: *a painting entitled, "The Landing of William Penn, 1682." Below: a 1702 view of Philadelphia.*

German and Welsh miners found iron ore and started iron works.

In 1701, the three Delaware counties demanded changes. The colonists said that Penn favored Pennsylvania. They wanted a separate government for Delaware. Penn agreed, and Delaware's first legislature met in 1704. The same governor served both colonies until the American Revolution.

With the founding of Pennsylvania and Delaware, there were twelve English colonies from Maine to Carolina. Fifty years passed before the last English colony was begun in the wilderness south of the Carolinas.

9

OGLETHORPE'S DREAM FOR GEORGIA

In London, a war hero named James Oglethorpe went to visit a friend who had been jailed for debt. Many people went to prison because they couldn't pay their bills. Oglethorpe knew that, but he had not known of the dirt, the smells, the foul food, or the diseases in the Fleet Street prison. His friend died of smallpox.

As a member of Parliament, Oglethorpe tried to change things. He and other lawmakers studied the prisons. Then they asked the government to start a new colony for London's poor.

In 1732, King George II granted a charter for a colony between the Savannah and Altamaha rivers. In the king's honor, it was named Georgia. The new colony was set up as a charity, and people all over England gave money to help.

Oglethorpe and thirty-five families sailed for Georgia in 1732. After they landed, most of the settlers waited in Charles Town while Oglethorpe and Colonel William Bull of South Carolina went south to find a settlement site. They chose a site a few miles inland from the mouth of the Savannah River.

As soon as the others arrived in February 1733, Oglethorpe put them to work building Savannah. A month later, a visitor reported that several houses were already built and that even the boys and girls were working hard. Oglethorpe laid out Savannah in squares, so every house could have a garden. Settlers had trouble getting used to the summer heat, but plants grew like wonders.

Before they began building, Oglethorpe had asked permission from local Indians. Chief Tomo-chi-chi of the Creek tribe became a good friend of the colony. Oglethorpe later traveled far inland exploring and making friends with other Indians. The Spanish and French attacked Georgia, but, because of Oglethorpe, settlers did not have to fight Indians. In fact, the Indians fought beside the settlers against the Spanish.

At first, the colony had high-minded rules. Heads of families got 50 acres (20 ha) of free land. No one was supposed to own more than 500 acres (200 ha). People were not to lose their land because

A portrait of James Oglethorpe, philanthropist, soldier, and founder of Georgia.

Slaves working in a rice field outside Savannah.

A RICE FIELD

of debt. One rule that did not last was the law banning slavery. By 1750, slavery became legal in Georgia.

Like Jamestown in its early years, Georgia ran on army rules. There was no governor and no elected assembly. General Oglethorpe gave the orders. He had forts built on St. Simons Island, on Cumberland Island, at the mouth of the St. Johns River, and inland on the Savannah River.

Though the first plan had been to settle poor Londoners in Georgia, the colony welcomed people from many countries. Among the early settlers were Germans and Scots. By 1741, the colony had about fourteen hundred settlers.

With the settlement of Georgia in 1733, thirteen English colonies formed an unbroken chain along the coast. From north to south, they were New Hampshire, Massachusetts, Rhode Island, Connecticut, New York, New Jersey, Pennsylvania, Delaware, Maryland, Virginia, North Carolina, South Carolina, and Georgia. These thirteen colonies united against England in 1776 to form the United States.

INDEX